599
S

**Schick, Alice**

**Serengeti cats**

| DATE | | | |
|---|---|---|---|
| APR 14 '78 | FEB 17 '88 | JAN 22 '98 | |
| MAY 23 '78 | FEB 24 '88 | MR 19 '99 | |
| OCT 27 '79 | MAR 19 '90 | AP 16 '00 | |
| | FEB 12 1992 | NOV 24 '99 | |
| | MAY 19 1992 | SEP 13 2000 | |
| | SEP 25 1992 | MAY 18 2000 | |
| SEP 22 '8 | SEP 29 1992 | OCT 0 2 20 | |
| SEP 30 '81 | NOV 20 1995 | NO 2 1 '05 | |
| OCT 8 '81 | MAY 08 '98 | | |
| JAN 22 '82 | MAY 14 '98 | DE 19 '05 | |
| FEB 13 '82 | SEP 04 '98 | DC 12 '06 | |
| NOV 24 '82 | SEP 11 '98 | MAR 12 2014 | |

© THE BAKER & TAYLOR CO.

# Serengeti Cats

# Serengeti Cats

## Alice Schick

*Illustrated by Joel Schick*

*J. B. Lippincott Company*

PHILADELPHIA AND NEW YORK

U.S. Library of Congress Cataloging in Publication Data

Schick, Alice.
  Serengeti cats.

  SUMMARY: Details the lives of lions, leopards, and cheetahs from birth
through adulthood in Tanzania's Serengeti National Park and describes
man's role in protecting the future of these cats.
  1. Lions.   2. Leopards.   3. Cheetahs.   4. Mammals—Tanzania—
Serengeti Plains.  5. Serengeti Plains, Tanzania. [1. Lions. 2. Leopards.
3. Cheetahs. 4. Serengeti Plains, Tanzania] I. Schick, Joel.
II. Title.
  QL737.C23S34      599'.74428      77-812
  ISBN-0-397-31757-3

*For Rover*

# Contents

*Chapter One*   The Serengeti   *13*

*Chapter Two*   Birth   *37*

*Chapter Three*   Growing Up   *69*

*Chapter Four*   Independence   *95*

*Chapter Five*   The Future for Serengeti Cats   *121*

# Serengeti Cats

*Chapter One*

# The Serengeti

Just south of the Equator, at the northern border of the East African country of Tanzania, lies an area called Serengeti. In the Swahili language the word Serengeti means grassy plain, and indeed, the Serengeti is essentially ten thousand square miles of grassland. A little more than half this area is a national park. The Serengeti National Park, which is just about the same size as the state of Connecticut, is home to millions of animals of hundreds of different species, and it is probably the most famous place in the world for natural-habitat wildlife viewing.

## Serengeti Cats

In a way, a visit to the Serengeti is like a journey to an earlier time, when *Homo sapiens* was a new species, just one of many whose very survival depended on whatever nature provided. Today, humans do not fit into the ecology of the Serengeti in quite the same way, but modern people have a far greater influence on its wildlife than their ancestors did. This story of lions, leopards and cheetahs is really the story of all the Serengeti's animals. It is the story of people too, for even now the lives of humans and animals are interdependent.

A January morning on the Serengeti. The sun, just up, gave little warmth and only an eerie, indistinct light in the thick fog. The land's physical features were enveloped in heavy mist. No wind blew and all seemed hushed and deserted.

An hour later the land was transformed. The equatorial sun, high in the sky, had burned off most of the fog. Stretching endlessly in every direction was the plain, covered with new grass wet with dew. Only a few trees, mostly flat-topped umbrella acacias, dotted the green sea. Here and there, a group of rocky hills known as kopjes broke the monotony of the landscape.

But the scenery was not the most compelling feature of the Serengeti this January morning, for the grassy plain teemed with animal life. Wildebeests, zebras, Thomson's gazelles by the thousands stood silently in the rising mists. So very many it seemed that there must be an animal for every blade of grass.

The vast herds had arrived in November, with the onset of the short rains. Overnight, following the first rain, new grass sprouted on the parched brown plains of the eastern Serengeti. Within a few days, the land was covered with nutritious young plants for the grass-eaters. When the animals arrived they found a carpet of food at their hooves.

The eastern short-grass plains were the traditional calving grounds for the gnus, zebras and Tommies. Most of the adult females who poured into the area were pregnant. During the last weeks before giving birth, they found abundant, high-quality food, a critical factor in the development of their unborn young. The well-nourished females generally gave birth to strong, healthy calves.

Nevertheless, many of the young herbivores born early in the season, while the rains of November and December lasted, did not survive. Predators could easily pick out a single newborn animal in a large

herd, and they took a huge toll. Only now, late in January, with the short rains just about over, were the births starting to peak. In a period of about six weeks, most of the calves would be born. Some of the relatively helpless creatures would lose their lives, but many thousands would not. There would be enough calves so that predators would not go hungry, and enough to insure the survival of each herbivore species.

Near the fringes of an enormous herd, a newborn wildebeest lay still on the wet grass, exhausted from the birth struggle. The mother gnu was exhausted also, but neither she nor her calf could rest now. The female began to lick her baby, carefully removing the fetal membranes, drying the newborn calf. She concentrated much of her attention on the calf's head, making sure that its breathing passages were clear and at the same time acquainting her baby with her own smell. A wildebeest calf that cannot identify its own mother in the herd by her smell will surely die.

The mother's licking stimulated the young gnu to make its first attempts to stand up. The baby began to kick its legs, but each limb seemed to have a life of its own and the gnu made little progress. The mother gently nudged the calf's rump, and this helped the baby coordinate the operations of its two front legs. It rose partway, but then the tiny hooves slipped and the calf sprawled on the grass. Luckily, the baby persisted, and after six unsuccessful efforts it stood triumphantly, if shakily, on four spindly legs.

The mother wildebeest moved a few paces away, encouraging her calf to follow. The baby did so, hesitantly at first, but gaining confidence with each shaky step. The mother did not move away again when her baby reached her, but stood calmly, allowing the calf to nuzzle her belly. The baby soon found a nipple and began to nurse.

The whole process took only twenty minutes. The newborn calf would have all day to gain strength and coordination. When evening came and the herd moved to its customary sleeping place, the little wildebeest would be able to follow. This baby would survive.

Not every newborn wildebeest was so lucky. Nearby, another calf was born. In spite of its mother's persistent prodding, it could not stand properly. When it tried to take a step, it lost its balance and fell. The mother stood watching it nervously all day, but at sunset she moved off with the herd. The calf was too weak to follow, and it lay at the spot where it was born, bleating softly. Within minutes, the deserted calf fell prey to a hyena.

All over the plain, the drama of birth was replayed ten thousand times a day. Zebra births were peaking too. Not far from their mothers, a pair of zebra foals played, frisking about on improbably long legs. Their new brown and white coats sparkled in the bright sunlight. The brown stripes would turn black in a few months.

Like the wildebeests', the young zebras' survival depended on their ability to follow their mothers almost from the instant of birth. At first they would follow anything that moved. But within a few days most could recognize their own mothers by sight and by smell.

Occasionally a zebra foal was too independent. One colt wandered far afield and became lost. His mother was nowhere in sight. But the foal's urge to follow was strong and he began to trot after two young male lions. The lions seemed to be strolling aimlessly rather than hunting. At first they seemed unaware of their unlikely pursuer, but as the zebra approached, one lion whirled about and charged. The foal was brought down with a quick swipe of a powerful paw.

The newborn young of the much smaller Thomson's gazelles had to learn a different survival pattern. This morning a young female was about to give birth for the first time. While the herd of delicate little antelopes stood in the sun, she moved off a short distance. She would have her baby alone, without the protection of the herd. The baby was born without incident and the female licked it dry. Within an hour the fawn was up and walking.

But the little Tommie did not follow its mother back to the herd. Its survival depended on staying put. Born with the urge to lie down in a protected place, the tiny gazelle settled into the first clump of bushes it found. Flat against the ground and unmoving, it was nearly invisible. It moved only when its mother called. After nursing, the baby returned to its hiding place while the mother returned to the herd to graze.

The mother Tommie never set foot in her fawn's hiding place. Her approach would have left her scent and drawn predators to the baby. The fawn itself had no odor, and the mother carefully cleaned away every speck of dirt from its coat while it nursed. Tucked away in its clump of bushes, the newborn Thomson's gazelle could not be detected by sight, hearing or smell. Predators passed within a few feet of its hiding place without noticing the fawn. It was safe as long as it stayed put and as long as nothing happened to its mother.

In the morning light, a regal-looking cat strolled across the plain. In some ways, the cheetah, called Duma in Swahili, was a rather uncatlike creature. She was taller and slimmer than cats of other species, and her head was smaller and rounder. Her long legs revealed her as a fast runner but a poor climber.

Despite her narrow, streamlined build and light weight of one hundred pounds, the cheetah was muscular and strong. With typical feline fastidiousness, she kept her tawny, black-spotted coat perfectly groomed. Her long tail, covered with spots near the base and circled by rings near the tip, was carried with the grace and confident attitude of a true cat.

Duma's favorite prey was Thomson's gazelle. She had followed the antelopes on their migration to the eastern Serengeti. There, where the gazelles gave birth to their fawns, in a few weeks the cheetah's own cubs would also be born.

While she awaited the birth of her young, the cheetah hunted every day. Usually she was successful. Young Tommies, just starting to move with the herd, had no experience with predators and presented little challenge to the speedy cat.

After walking awhile, Duma lay down next to a bush. She was relaxed but alert. Her amber eyes scanned the horizon, missing nothing. To the west, six giraffes browsed leisurely on some thorn trees. They seemed to relish the dry, needle-sharp spines. A black rhinoceros lay on its side in a mud wallow. Three ostriches sauntered by.

The cheetah was looking for a meal. She picked out a gazelle grazing by itself. Duma stood up slowly and stretched. She began to walk toward the Tommie. The gazelle was alert too and saw the cat approaching. But the cat was three hundred feet away, too far to cause flight. The gazelle began to graze again and Duma, knowing that she had been seen, settled down to rest.

For the next three hours the cheetah licked herself, swatted at flies and waited. The gazelle looked up from the grass once in a while, but seeing that the cat had not moved, continued to eat. Then, almost casually, Duma stood up. The Tommie saw this, but the cheetah did not appear to be hunting and remained too far away to cause fear.

Suddenly, without warning, the cheetah began to run. In a second the critical gap of safety between predator and prey was closed. The gazelle took off. But over a short distance it was no match for Duma, who could hit the speed of seventy miles an hour.

The cheetah quickly overtook the gazelle, knocking it over with a blow of a front paw. When the prey was down, Duma gripped its neck in her jaws, cutting vital blood vessels and crushing the windpipe. Death came swiftly.

Duma began to feed. Within minutes, a great horde of vultures, of five different species, descended on the scene of the kill. Cheetahs will sometimes abandon their kills to vultures, but Duma was hungry and she growled and slapped at the birds when they got too close. She seemed to realize, though, that she must quickly eat her fill. Other predators, larger and more powerful than the cheetah, watch the skies to see where vultures congregate. No cheetah will defend its kill against a lion or a hyena. The risk of being hurt is too great. Even a slight injury which slows a cheetah just a little can mean hunting failure and slow starvation.

So Duma ate and then trotted off, leaving half her kill to the vultures and to the hyenas who soon appeared to chase the birds away. Twelve hours after the kill, all traces of the Thomson's gazelle were gone.

Not far from this scene, a tiny gazelle fawn lay motionless in a thicket, waiting for a signal from its mother. So well was the fawn hidden that a lion passed not six feet away without seeing it. But as the hours went by, the little gazelle grew anxious and hungry. It could not know that its mother had been killed by a cheetah, and even if it could have understood, the outcome would have been the same. A fawn cannot survive without its mother. Finally, the little gazelle left the thicket and almost at once it was discovered.

The Tommie fawn was tiny, but it was a big kill for the golden jackal, whose usual diet was composed largely of insects. The jackal ate his fill, then buried the rest of the carcass. When he returned to his den, he regurgitated part of his meal for his mate and their pups, who were just beginning to eat solid food.

To the west of the grassy plain where the cheetah hunted gazelles, the Serengeti is more wooded. Stands of acacia trees, gently rolling hills and shrub-covered kopjes give the area an almost planned, park-like appearance. At the border between grassland and woodland stands a small settlement called Seronera.

Seronera is the headquarters of the Serengeti National Park, the base of operations for the park rangers, for many of the scientists studying East African plants and animals and for the thousands of tourists who visit the Serengeti.

Near Seronera, in the heat of the January afternoon, a young lioness relaxed on a kopje in the shade of a huge candelabra euphorbia tree. In contrast to the cheetah, Simba (as the lion is called in Swahili) was a typical feline. Her paws were big and powerful, her jaws strong. She was built for strength rather than speed, although all her motions were flowing and graceful. Sprawled on her side, the tawny cat dozed, unmoving except for the black-tufted tip of her tail, which twitched with a life of its own. To a tourist who watched her, Simba looked surprisingly like a three-hundred-pound house cat napping away the warm afternoon.

Not far away, two lionesses licked each other companionably, while on the opposite side of the kopje, several young lions slept together in a confused jumble of paws, heads and tails. All seven of the adult lionesses in the pride were there, along with six cubs of differing ages and one of the pride's three

27

adult males. The group's size would soon be increased, for in a few weeks Simba and another lioness would both have cubs.

The cats moved little during the long afternoon. They paid no attention to a brief rain shower or to a carload of tourists who stopped to watch and take pictures. Since the center of the pride's home range was so near Seronera, the animals were quite used to people. Even the cubs ignored the tourists' cars.

At dusk the cats began to stir. Simba stood up, stretched, yawned and walked over to another lioness. The two rubbed cheeks in greeting, then settled down to groom each other. A couple of animals ambled away, as if out for an evening stroll. The cubs played.

An hour later Simba and three other lionesses left the kopje, walking slowly in the direction of the Seronera River. They were searching for prey, but there was no apparent sense of urgency in their actions. The cats behaved as if they had no intention of walking any great distance. They seemed to be waiting for some suitable prey to cross their path. Often the lionesses stopped to look around and listen.

A large bull buffalo emerged from a thicket. He was an impressive animal in the prime of life. The bull's coat was black and shiny in the moonlight. His skull was massive, with heavy, downward-curving horns growing out of the broad forehead.

The lionesses fanned out and began to approach the buffalo at a stalk. Suddenly, Simba was directly in front of him. She hesitated. This "prey" was several times her size and not at all defenseless. It is just about impossible for a single lioness to bring down a healthy, mature bull buffalo. Even if the other three lionesses joined in the attack, their chances of success would not be good.

As for the buffalo, he had faced lions before. Like many others of his species, he carried on his shoulders old scars from an attack by a lion, proof that buffalo are formidable prey for the big cats. Now he stood his ground. When Simba stepped forward, the buffalo lowered his head, waving his horns menacingly. He was quite capable of killing a lion with either his horns or his hooves.

The situation was a standoff. The lionesses seemed to realize that the buffalo was dangerous. After only twenty minutes they walked off. Perhaps if they had been hungrier they would not have given up so easily. But only two days earlier they had chased some vultures from the remains of a giraffe and gorged themselves on some other predators' kill.

Like all lions, Simba was an opportunist about food. She would kill her own prey if necessary, but scavenged if she could. She was not fussy about freshness. If a kill was large, she and other members of her pride would feed off it for several days, guarding the carcass between meals. The meat she scavenged did not have to be fresh either. Nor did she have to eat every day. Stimulated by competition from the other lions, Simba could consume fifty pounds of meat or more at a single meal. If she then went a week without eating again, she would not be hungry.

Simba and her companions soon settled down in the grass. During the night they wandered around for short periods and made two more casual attempts at hunting, but they did not kill anything.

The Serengeti National Park headquarters is named for the nearby river, the Seronera. Because the Seronera is a permanent river, with water even during the long dry season, its banks support dense vegetation. Yellow-barked fever trees are common there, and much of the ground is covered with tangled thickets of bushes. The riverine forest near the park headquarters was the home of Chui, the leopard.

Chui was only half the size of a lioness, but proportionately stronger. Like the lion, she had large heavy paws and a good-sized head with powerful jaws. Her spots were not really spots at all, but rosettes—open, irregular circles of brown and black on her pale coat. The underside of her long tail was white.

The leopard was a solitary cat, more secretive than the cheetah or lion. Most tourists who visited the Serengeti would never have seen Chui but for the sharp eyes of their African guides. The park rangers could pick out the most perfectly camouflaged wildlife, including the leopard reclining on a tree branch. In the tree, Chui's rosettes broke up her outline, making her beautiful coat blend with the sun-dappled leaves. To find her, the rangers counted on a knowledge of her habits and looked for the long white tip of her tail dangling below a branch.

Lately, Chui had been harder to find than usual. While she was normally quite calm about the tourists who watched her, she would soon have cubs. Until the babies were big enough to move around and climb trees on their own, she would keep them hidden. Now she was spending her time in the thickest

part of the riverine forest, where she would select a
site for her den.

In the warm afternoon Chui lay on a horizontal
branch, her front paws stretched out before her and
her back legs dangling, one on either side of the
branch. It was a comical pose, and only a leopard
could have managed to look dignified in such a position.

Chui dozed, every now and then opening her eyes
to look around slowly. She yawned, seemingly taking
great pleasure in the simple act, stretching her jaws
wide and extending her tongue. A small dark rain
cloud moved rapidly across the sky, dropping a brief,
gentle shower on the leopard's tree. The water
brought Chui fully awake.

Purposefully, the cat climbed down the tree
trunk, moving headfirst. She flowed silently through
the undergrowth, disappearing in the bushes. She
was hunting, heading for a place along the river's
edge favored by reedbuck, a water-loving antelope
that formed an important part of her diet.

In a stand of tall grass and bushes, three impalas
stood browsing. During the dry season, these antelopes would gather in large herds near the rivers. But
now, at the end of the short rains, they were scat-

tered in small groups throughout the woodlands. Chui began to stalk the impalas, trotting a short distance crouched low to the ground, then freezing, then moving again. But before she got close enough to spring, the impalas sensed her presence and leaped away.

Chui did not follow, instead resuming her search for reedbuck. She checked four places before she found her quarry, a reedbuck crouched in some tall grass. The leopard stalked carefully, slowly, quietly. If possible she would move in right next to the animal. She was not nearly as quick as an antelope, so she could not run it down. It might even escape in the time it took her to spring. The leopard's best weapon was stealth, and now it served her well. The reedbuck remained unaware of her until it was too late. The leopard seized the antelope's throat in her jaws. The reedbuck did not even struggle. Like many prey animals, it went into a state of shock at the predator's touch and did not suffer as it died of strangulation.

Chui did not eat her prey on the spot. Instead, she began to drag it through the tall grass to her tree. Her strength was so great that she was able to climb forty feet up a vertical tree trunk carrying an antelope of nearly her own weight in her jaws. Even so, the process was tiring, and bringing home her kill took longer than the hunt.

Finally the reedbuck was stored securely in the tree, safe from lions, who were unlikely to notice it and less likely to climb up after it even if they did see it. Vultures too were unlikely to bother the kill, although they could reach it more easily than lions. The leopard would be able to have several meals from this carcass, so she did not have to gorge herself now. In fact, the reedbuck would last her nearly a week, and Chui would not hunt again until it was gone unless a very good opportunity presented itself. When she was finished with the carcass, anything that was left would fall from the tree, to be consumed by ground-dwelling scavengers.

Chui ate her first meal from the evening's kill. Afterward, she sat on the branch and washed herself slowly and very thoroughly. Then, in spite of the leopard's reputation for prowling at night, Chui settled down on the branch, her head resting on her front paws, and slept until dawn.

*Chapter Two*

# Birth

There is a rhythm to the seasons on the Serengeti, a rhythm set by the rains. In most years the short dry season of January and February is followed by the long rains of March, April and May. During these three months, as much as half of the Serengeti's annual rain falls.

The long rains mean overcast skies, swollen streams, impassable mudholes where once there were dirt roads. Understandably, few tourists visit the Serengeti at this time of year. For the animals, however, the rainy season is a time of welcome abundance. A fresh carpet of grass means food for thousands of newly weaned herbivores. And many healthy, well-fed young plant-eaters mean that predators can hunt successfully. There is enough food for the adults and enough to feed young meat-eaters. So, although predators may give birth at any time of year, the spring rainy season is probably the best time of year for young carnivores to be born.

It was early on a March morning that the rains began. Most of the lions in Simba's pride were sheltered under a tree, but they did not really seem bothered by the water. In fact, they seemed to enjoy the refreshing rain. Several adults and near-adults frisked about, swatting at flies or charging at waving blades of grass. Like all lions, they were more playful and kittenish during the rainy season.

Most lions roam farther than usual during the rains. On this morning, two cats from a neighboring pride were strolling far from home. Actually, they were within the area occupied by their pride, but far from its center. Their pride used this piece of land very little because it was also part of the area used by Simba's pride. Although the loosely defined, frequently shifting territories of prides often overlap, the cats generally avoid confronting strange lions. So

when the intruders roared, they were answered with roars from the area's usual inhabitants, and they immediately turned around and trotted back home. The lions never met Simba's pride face to face.

One member of the pride who did not roar to help drive the strangers away was Simba. This morning she was busy with other matters. During the night she had gone off alone and found an isolated dip in the ground, bordered by tall grass. There she lay down and slept until she was awakened by the first contractions of labor.

Within an hour, four cubs—two males and two females—were born. It was Simba's first litter but she seemed to know just what to do, cleaning and drying each cub and guiding it to a nipple to nurse.

The newborn cubs were small—about three pounds each—and totally helpless. They were toothless, their eyes were shut tight and, for the first day of life, they could not even crawl. Their woolly yellow fur was covered with dark spots which would fade as they grew up but which, for now, helped to camouflage the kittens. The cubs' survival depended completely on Simba's skill at keeping them concealed, warm and well-fed.

*       *       *

On the same day, under a tangle of bushes near the Seronera River, the leopard Chui also gave birth. There were three cubs. Two, a male and a female, were strong and healthy, each weighing over a pound. The third was a runt, only half the others' size. Its movements were feeble and its cries weak. Unlike its siblings, it did not struggle eagerly to feed. Within hours it died, and Chui picked up the tiny body and removed it from the den.

Many wild leopards die within the first few weeks after birth. In a way, it was lucky that this runty cub had died so quickly. Now Chui's milk would be divided between only two kittens. Later, when the cubs started to eat meat, each would receive a larger share. With only two cubs, the mother leopard, who would have to provide for her offspring by herself, had a good chance of raising them to maturity.

But on this day maturity seemed a long way off. The kittens were blind and toothless. Their fur looked longer, woollier and paler than their mother's, and their spots were small, not yet standing out strikingly against the background color. There was no hint from their appearance that these tiny creatures would ever grow into strong, graceful hunters like Chui.

## Serengeti Cats

All day the mother leopard lay in the den with her newborn cubs, contentedly dozing, allowing the kittens to nurse and licking them gently with a tongue that covered a tiny body in one swipe. No human observer, not even the sharpest-eyed park ranger, could have seen the leopard family. It was the perfect place for a den.

At nightfall, Chui crept out of the den to hunt. She was gone only long enough to catch and eat a large hare. Yet it was long enough for her cubs to miss her warm, comforting presence. They began to call for her, making soft *urr-urr* sounds.

The kittens' crying attracted the attention of a serval, a small spotted cat with unusually large ears. The serval was hunting, using its ability to rotate each ear separately and its acute hearing to locate prey it couldn't see in the tall, dense vegetation. The serval was about to investigate the sounds in the thicket when Chui returned. In the face of a leopard, the noises did not seem very interesting. Forgetting about a potential meal, the serval ran, disappearing with a series of great leaps through the underbrush.

The leopard did not pursue the smaller cat. She was far more interested in the safety of her cubs. The cubs, completely unaware of how close they had

come to being killed, were still calling for their mother and did not stop crying until Chui had entered the den and lay curled around them.

The leopard cubs may have been content, but their mother knew she could no longer keep her family in the thicket. She picked up one of the cubs, handling it just as a domestic cat carries a kitten, with the loose skin of the cub's neck held gently in her teeth. Warily, she left the thicket and headed toward the river. She padded down a slight incline, slipping silently into the water. The river was not very wide, but because of the rain the water was high and Chui was forced to swim. She kept the front of her body well out of the water so the cub in her mouth would not be dunked. Once across, she headed surely for a hollow tree and set the cub down inside.

Then she swam back across the river, retrieved the second cub and repeated the whole procedure. Four trips across the river meant a lot of swimming for an animal who preferred to avoid water. But Chui, like most leopards, was a very protective mother, and she seemed to know that the serval would not cross the river. Now, in the hollow tree, her family was once again safely hidden.

\* \* \*

*Birth*

Farther east, on the grassy, open plain, the time drew near for the birth of the cheetah's young. Duma did not like the rain. Running down prey was more difficult on muddy, slippery ground, and it was only because there were so many young antelopes that the cheetah was able to find enough to eat.

Out on the open plain, the cheetah did not have as great a selection of den sites as the leopard in the riverine forest. Nevertheless, Duma thoroughly inspected all the possibilities before choosing a large, spreading thorny acacia bush. Under the tangle of prickly branches, the cheetah gave birth to three tiny cubs, two males and a female.

The cheetah's cubs were very small, about half a pound each in weight, and, at birth, looked very little like the cats they would grow up to be. Where their mother's fur was short and coarse, the cubs had long, fluffy blue-gray manes on their heads, shoulders and backs. Under the long hair, their coats were smoky gray, not tawny yellow, and their spots looked fuzzy and indistinct. Unlike adult cheetahs, who cannot retract their claws in the manner of other cats, the cheetah cubs had usable claw sheaths. By the time they were four months old, the claw sheaths would disappear. But for now, the cubs' retractile claws made nursing a more comfortable process for their mother, since the kittens kneaded her side with their front paws as they fed.

Like other newborn cats, the baby cheetahs were quite helpless. Their eyes were closed, their ears looked like little bumps on the sides of their heads and they could not stand up. And like other cat mothers, Duma seemed to be aware of her cubs' vulnerability. In their first few days of life, she hardly left the den. Her appetite was reduced and she did not hunt. She seemed content to lie with her young, feeding them and cleaning them, purring loudly all the while.

Duma could purr like a domestic cat because her throat structure was similar to a domestic cat's. She could not roar like a lion or leopard, whose internal throat structure makes them incapable of purring. Even without a roar, however, the range of noises made by a cheetah is astonishing. Duma was a vocal cat, and in the long process of rearing her cubs, she would make use of nearly her whole vocabulary.

By the time the cheetah cubs were a week old they had gained enough strength to be moved. Duma selected a new den under another thorny acacia bush, and, one by one, she carried the still-blind cubs to

their new home. The next day, the kittens opened their eyes, and by the time they were two weeks old they could stand up and walk well. Duma continued to change dens every few days, probably to prevent discovery of her young by predators as well as to keep the cubs in a clean place. When the cubs were three weeks old she stopped carrying them. Now when they moved, the three little cheetahs followed their mother, trotting along by themselves. They moved in single file, Duma keeping them in line by calling to them, *prrr-prrr*.

The cheetah cubs were very obedient. Although they grew more playful and energetic every day, they would remain quietly in the den for hours when their mother was out hunting. Duma would call to her cubs in a chirping voice to let them know she was coming home. The kittens would answer in higher chirps that sounded exactly like birds' voices, calling their mother excitedly, but still not leaving the den without her permission. As soon as Duma entered, the cubs tumbled all over her in happy excitement, jumping up, standing on their hind legs, embracing her with their front paws, licking her face.

It was difficult for kittens who greeted their mother with such enthusiasm after a short separation to keep from following her whenever she left. Yet they always obeyed her vocal command to stay put. A baby cheetah who ignored orders would not survive for long on the Serengeti. Those cheetahs born with the tendency to obey their mothers are likely to live long enough to grow up. Those cheetahs born without that tendency are likely to die young. Over the course of many thousands of years, this useful trait for survival has become concentrated in the cheetah population, so that most wildborn cheetahs have it.

Duma's young grew fast. By the time they were three weeks old and moving about by themselves, they had also begun teething. Their milk teeth were small, but they were like little needles and would serve the cubs well until they got their permanent teeth at the age of eight months. The milk teeth were sufficiently sharp and strong to allow the cubs to begin experimenting with meat-eating, which they did about two weeks later.

The first time Duma brought a haunch of her kill for her young, she called them out of the den and dropped the meat in front of them. One cub hung back, unwilling even to investigate the strange object. The second approached warily and sniffed the meat, but then jumped up with a hiss. Only the third was really interested, but she could not break through the skin. When Duma opened a hole for her, the cub began to eat hungrily. She would not stop until Duma nipped her, to prevent the cub from eating too much.

Within a few days, the male cheetah cubs were eating meat along with their sister. The young cheetahs would continue to nurse until they were three months old, but with each day meat became a more important part of their diet.

With the cubs eating meat, Duma had to hunt more. Once in a while she was helped by a large, dark-colored male cheetah who was the cubs' father. When she hunted with her mate, Duma usually selected larger prey than she was willing to tackle alone. One day the two cheetahs brought down a full-grown wildebeest, which provided more than enough food for them and the cubs. Occasionally, the male cheetah brought part of a kill he had made by himself to feed his family. But male cheetahs have no permanent ties to females and no firm responsibilities for cubs. For the most part, Duma provided for her cubs alone.

As soon as the little cheetahs could walk well, they began to accompany their mother on hunting expeditions. Following obediently in a line, they would sit down at a signal from Duma when she had spotted her prey. They waited, watching while their mother made the kill, learning by observation some of the hunting skills they would soon need for survival. When Duma returned with their meal, the cubs waited until she gave them the *prrr-prrr* signal to come and eat. Even if she ate first, as she often did, the little cheetahs waited patiently until Duma allowed them to take their share.

Throughout the spring rainy season, the cheetah family lived contentedly on the eastern Serengeti. Food was abundant, numerous thorny bushes provided shelter, and few lions occupied the area. Duma could keep her cubs healthy, well-fed and safe. But the season changed. The rains lessened and the land began to dry out. By the middle of May, when the cheetah cubs were two months old, the vibrant green of the grasses had faded. Here and there in the light green sea, a patch of yellow or brown was visible, a sure sign of the coming summer dry season. Water holes and intermittent streams dried up, and Duma would sometimes leave her cubs in the den while she walked great distances for a drink.

Cheetahs can survive easily in dry areas. Since they do not stalk their prey like leopards, they do not need the cover of tall grass or bushes for hunting.

## Serengeti Cats

Barren ground suits their running style. Neither do they need water holes or streams. They will drink if water is available, but if necessary they can get all the moisture they need from their prey. The one problem Duma would have during the dry season would be finding enough food for herself and her cubs.

Unlike the cheetahs, most of the hoofed animals could not tolerate the dried-out grasslands. They needed green grass to eat and water to drink. Each year, at the beginning of the long dry season, the great herds would begin a westward migration, moving toward the woodland. There they could find grass that was still green as well as permanent water holes and streams. Even in the wetter, more wooded areas, the dry season was a difficult time for the herbivores. Many would not survive. But their chances for survival were greater where there was more food and water, and so they moved, along migration routes thousands of years old, first the zebras and the wildebeests, then the Thomson's gazelles.

By July, most of the hoofed animals would be gone. Instead of the thousands upon thousands of herbivores that occupied the eastern Serengeti during the rains, there would be only a few Tommies, some

Grant's gazelles, and ostriches. A single adult cheetah might be able to find enough food here, but a mother cat with three growing, hungry cubs could not. And so, in late June, Duma left the cubs' birthplace and led her offspring west, toward Seronera, following the herds.

The kittens were three months old now and looked almost like miniature adult cheetahs. The long mantles of hair on their backs had almost disappeared, leaving only small wiry manes on their necks. Their coats had turned tawny, with well-defined spots. The female cub was the smallest of the three, but she was the most mature and adventurous. She seemed to be the leader of the cubs. The two males could be distinguished from each other by both color and temperament. One was rather dark like his father. The other was light in color, his spots standing out vividly against a cream-colored background. The light-colored cub was the shyest of the three, often hanging back from some adventure until he was reassured by his brother.

In their new home near Seronera, the cheetah family found a perfect playground—a colony of termite hills. East African termites build cone-shaped dirt houses more than ten feet high. As far as the young cheetahs were concerned, these termite hills were designed for their enjoyment. The cubs dashed around madly, zigzagging among the mounds. They charged up the termite hills. They used the mounds as hiding places, one cub crouching behind a hill, then pouncing on another cub as it walked past. Most often they chased each other, with one cub swatting at another as if it were prey. This type of play, like watching their mother hunt, helped to train the young cheetahs for life on their own.

One day Duma caught a small gazelle but did not kill it. Instead, she brought it to her cubs and dropped it in front of them. At first the young cheetahs seemed afraid, but then the female walked over and batted it tentatively. At this, the gazelle jumped up and ran. All three cubs chased it, unsuccessfully. Although the dark male knocked it down once, the gazelle got up and ran away again. It was soon obvious that the cubs could not catch the prey, and Duma quickly brought it down herself.

The whole family then ate, companionably sharing the prey. There was no growling or squabbling. The light-colored male cub did not object even when his sister snatched a large, meaty bone from between his paws. Minutes later he simply took it back with

no argument from her. When the meal was over,
Duma and her cubs lay down among the termite
hills, licking one another and purring happily.

During the long rains, while the cheetah cubs
were learning about their environment, Simba's lion
cubs were developing too. At first the four little lions
had contact with no one but their mother. When
Simba was with them in the grassy hollow that
formed their den, the cubs *miaowed* for attention,
squabbled amongst themselves, nursed and slept.
Often, however, they were left alone. Like almost all
lions, Simba was a highly social creature and even the
demands of motherhood did not make her forget her
usual companions. Nearly every evening she returned
to the pride to take part in a hunt. Sometimes she left
the cubs during daylight hours just to spend time
with other lions.

While the cubs were alone they were vulnerable
to all kinds of danger. They survived because the den
was well-hidden, because they usually kept quiet
when their mother was not around and because, as
soon as they could move, they would crawl under a
rock at the first unfamiliar noise. Many small lion
cubs die while their mothers are away. Some cry at

just the wrong moment when a predator is passing by. Some are abandoned by their mother when her desire to remain with the pride is too strong. Simba's cubs were lucky. Their mother always returned to take care of them.

By the time the little lions were five weeks old, they were healthy, playful kittens who would bounce out of the den to greet their mother when she grunted to them. They were so eager to follow her that Simba often had trouble making them stay in one place. Sometimes she led them into a tangle of bushes and then left quietly, moving too fast for the cubs to follow. At last even this trick did not work and Simba gave in, encouraging the cubs to follow her closely by grunting and moving slowly.

She led the cubs to the remains of an impala that she and another lioness had killed the previous evening. The cubs were interested in the meat and could have eaten it, since they already had most of their milk teeth, but they did not get much of a chance. The two lionesses had eaten most of the antelope by themselves. Besides, the other lioness was still on the carcass, and neither she nor Simba would stand by politely while the cubs got their share. Both adults growled and slapped at the cubs when they tried to eat, just as they growled and slapped at each other. And so the cubs learned their first lesson about life in a lion pride: You eat only what you can take.

The four cubs got almost no meat during that first meal. One little female managed to grab a scrap of skin from the kill. This became a toy and for a while the cubs played, chasing each other and biting at the prize, temporarily distracted from their main goal.

It was not important for the cubs to obtain meat this time because they still got all the nourishment they needed from their mother's milk. But they were growing rapidly and meat would become an increasingly important part of their diet. They would get the meat they needed only as part of the pride. When they were seven weeks old and could walk for extended periods without resting, Simba took her cubs to meet the rest of the pride. Other than the lioness who had snarled at them at the impala kill, the cubs had never seen an adult lion except their mother.

So very many lions! The cubs quickly learned which animals would stand for insults from youngsters. The adult males generally ignored cubs but were usually tolerant of small ones. Very young cubs could even get away with using the tail tufts of the big males as toys. Most of the lionesses accepted even

greater indignities before they threatened overly obnoxious cubs with snarls.

The pride now contained twelve cubs: six older juveniles from three different litters, Simba's four and two more, the survivors of a litter born a week before Simba's. All the lionesses seemed to share all the cubs. Mothers were content to nurse other cubs along with their own young. The big cubs whose mothers no longer had milk took advantage of the situation by nursing from lionesses who did. Simba's cubs survived this competition because she chased the older cubs away if they seemed to be preventing her own youngsters from getting food.

By the time the dry season began, Simba's four cubs were fully integrated into the pride, entitled like all the others to the protection and affection it afforded. Although the cubs were far too young to participate in hunts, they were entitled as well to fight for a share of the kills.

Chui's two leopard cubs, living on the bank of the Seronera River, were growing also. When they were three months old, they were weaned. They had developed the necessary strength and coordination to leave the den area and follow their mother.

The rate of the leopards' physical development was comparable to that of the lion cubs. But becoming an adult cat is more than a physical process—it is a learning process too. Unlike the lion cubs, who were learning from all the members of the pride, the leopard cubs had only their mother to teach them just what it meant to be an adult cat.

The little leopards watched their mother closely. When Chui walked through the tall grass, she carried her tail high in the air, exposing its white underside. By watching the moving white spot, the cubs could follow her easily. They learned to sit quietly while Chui hunted, having discovered by experience that even the smallest sound or movement from them would alert the prey and spoil the hunt.

The cubs also learned patience from watching their mother, who often observed her prey for hours before attacking. One day while they were playing near the den, the two cubs caught sight of a squirrel as it scurried across a nearby rock. Instantly the cubs crouched, eyes fixed on the squirrel. The squirrel sensed something, sat up and froze. For forty minutes the cubs watched the squirrel, their bodies tense with excitement, the tips of their tails twitching. The squirrel did not move at all.

Suddenly the male cub could stand it no longer and he rushed at the squirrel, his sister following. Of course, the rodent had been aware of the kittens, and it darted away so quickly that when the cubs pounced on the rock they were surprised to find nothing at all under their paws. The next time they would know that a leopard must wait until its prey moves into a more favorable position. It would be longer before they learned not to waste so much time waiting for such a small meal.

Very early in life the leopards became adept tree climbers. In their main home tree, the cubs were easy to watch, and Chui kept an eye on them, making sure they stayed out of trouble. She fed them in the tree, frequently bringing a separate kill for each cub. That way there was not much squabbling over food. When the kittens did fight over a piece of meat, as often as not the better portion fell to the ground and no one got any.

In July the dry season reached its peak. Day after day the sun shone brightly in a vast expanse of cloudless sky. An east wind blew almost continually, rustling the dry brown grasses, making the dust rise in little swirls. The grasslands had dried out first, and now the woodlands became tinder-dry too. Fires

started in the brush and blackened hundreds of acres before burning out. Only near the permanent rivers did green vegetation remain. More and more animals moved toward Seronera, seeking water and shady relief from the burning sun. This was the height of the tourist season, when Serengeti roads were passable and when wildlife in abundance could be found close to the lodges.

The three cats and their young were often seen by visitors, and they soon became popular attractions. Once the cubs could move around, the mother cats, who were all used to tourists, were less secretive. They generally remained in one place long enough for people to take all the photographs they wanted.

Although Duma the cheetah was indifferent to humans, she remained exceptionally alert for lions and was very nervous when they were near. Cheetah cubs are often killed by lions, and Duma seemed to be aware of the danger the larger cats posed to her three active kittens. She did her best to keep her family away from lions. In spite of her vigilance, she was forced by the distribution of prey animals to remain near Seronera, right in the middle of the territory of Simba's pride. A confrontation between the cheetah family and a lion was just about inevitable.

Late on an August afternoon Duma killed an impala fawn. As she carried it to her cubs, who were waiting nearby, Simba appeared from the opposite direction. The cheetah froze in her tracks. The lioness, who was alone, having left her cubs with other members of the pride, advanced without hesitation. She moved confidently, seemingly sure of her power, as if she had every right to take the cheetah's kill.

Sensing the lioness' determination, Duma seemed to realize that she could not defend her kill. She dropped the fawn and moved away, placing herself between the lioness and her cubs. But although she had given up the hard-won meal for her family, she would not give it up without a protest. As Simba stood sniffing and pawing the tiny antelope, Duma circled the lioness slowly at a distance of forty feet, all the while making growling and hissing noises. Twice she lunged at Simba, as if to take back the kill.

Duma probably knew that she could not take the fawn away from a lion, but she could not allow Simba to remain so close to her cubs. The cheetah would not leave the lioness alone so she could eat and finally Simba gave up, leaving the area at a trot. Unfortunately for Duma, she took the impala fawn with her.

\*     \*     \*

During the long dry season, births among the Serengeti's warthogs reach a peak. Within a few weeks of birth the homely little piglets are able to trot across the plain as nimbly as their parents. Serengeti tourists are sometimes treated to the sight of a whole family of warthogs—mother, father and half a dozen little ones—trotting through the dry grass in single file, their brush-tipped tails held stiffly in the air.

The lion cubs too were sometimes treated to this sight and it seemed to fascinate them. One family of warthogs made its home near the lion pride's favorite kopje. The cubs learned to wait for the warthogs to come out of their burrow and then, as the parents and their five piglets trotted away, to charge at them. The cubs were far too young and clumsy to catch anything, but it was fun to watch the warthogs scatter in every direction.

Simba's cubs played their game several times before the rules were suddenly changed. One day the warthog family had had enough. When the lions dashed at them, the father, a huge boar with large, menacing tusks, charged. Now it was the cats who turned tail and scattered. One cub, seeing the boar chasing him, panicked. He continued to run, even after the warthog family had regrouped and trotted away.

When the lion cub finally stopped running, he found himself under a tree, all alone, farther from his littermates than he had ever been. He began to *miaow*, crying loudly. Simba heard him but could not see him. She got up from her resting place and began to move toward the sound.

Another cat also heard the cub's frightened cries. Chui the leopard was resting in the tree above the lion. To her, the lost cub represented an easy meal. Silently, she climbed down the tree trunk and grabbed the lion cub by the throat. At that moment Simba appeared. Without hesitation, Chui dropped the cub and scampered back up the tree. But it was too late. The cub was dead. Simba sniffed it and pawed it. After a while, when it did not move, she turned away and walked slowly back to her three surviving cubs.

## Chapter Three

# Growing Up

The interminable dry season dragged on. Even in the woodlands water holes dried up, their beds turning to hardened, cracked mud. The Serengeti herbivores had difficulty finding enough green grass. They crowded into the narrow strips of land bordering the rivers, where some vegetation remained.

The wildebeest herds needed water, and every two or three days made their way nervously to the bank of the Seronera River to drink. They recognized that danger awaited them in the thickets near their watering place. For the dense cover favored the lion and the leopard, and Simba and Chui found the hunting good.

The leopard, of course, was permanently at home along the river. If there had not been large wildebeest calves available to her, she would have hunted something else. Like all leopards, she was adaptable, and her two cubs would not starve. The little leopards, well-fed and protected, were endlessly playful. They chased their own tails, each other and forest lizards. They leaped into the air, trying to catch butterflies. Every day their motions became more coordinated and graceful. And they began to cut their permanent teeth. In every way the cubs were preparing for the time when they would be independent adults.

Every day, new experiences taught the young leopards something about their environment. They learned which animals that shared their habitat were prey and which were dangerous. Once the cubs watched, wide-eyed, as a family of elephants came down to the river. While the other adult females and their calves drank and sprayed themselves and bathed, the leader, an enormous old female with a broken tusk, stood guard. Always alert, she stationed herself in the river, sniffing the air. She was fully aware of the two excited leopard cubs sneaking

through the bushes to get a better look. As soon as
the cubs crossed some invisible boundary, she trum-
peted and charged through the water, her ears held
out from the sides of her head and her trunk waving.
The leopard cubs didn't need their mother's call to
get them home. They turned tail and ran. Clearly,
these elephants were the dangerous kind.

The extended dry season caused the lion pride to
focus its activities along the Seronera River. The cats
were less inclined to wander than they were during
the rains, and with their prey concentrated near the
river, they had little reason to visit the more open
portions of their territory. Wildebeests were plentiful
and easily ambushed while they drank.

In some dry seasons the wildebeest herds selected
a different part of the woodlands. Then the lion pride
was forced to concentrate on hunting Thomson's gazelles. Each of these animals is so small that it makes
a meal for only one lioness, with little meat left over
for her cubs. Yet once she has eaten, a lioness has no
incentive to hunt again. Under these conditions, her
young almost invariably starve. And these conditions
happen often enough that starvation is the leading

cause of death among the 50 percent of all wild lion cubs who fail to survive.

Luckily for Simba's cubs, this was a good dry season. With the adult lions hunting large prey like wildebeests, there was almost always meat left for the cubs. Simba's three offspring remained fat and healthy.

The surviving male cub was easily distinguishable from his sisters. At the age of seven months, he still had no traces of a mane, but his face was already broader and his body more massive than the females'. At about this time, Simba's milk dried up. The cubs occasionally suckled from another lioness, but both she and Simba tolerated their attempts to nurse less and less often. In this way the cubs were weaned.

Still another pride lioness had given birth in August, and in October she brought her four young cubs to join the pride. The cats now seemed to consider the size of the pride too large. The adult cats began to behave aggressively toward two three-year-old females. Although these two littermates had been born and had grown up in the pride, suddenly they were no longer accepted. Their attempts to rub against other lions were met with growls and slaps.

They were chased away from kills. They were not permitted to rest near the cubs or the other adults.

Over a period of several weeks the two lionesses spent less and less time with the group. They began to hunt for themselves instead of trying to share in the others' kills. But then their former companions began to chase them away from their own kills. The pride members did not seem to want them in their territory. At last the two lionesses left the area, moving eastward. Perhaps they would join another pride; perhaps they would meet a male lion and start a new pride in a new territory; perhaps they would become nomads, wandering around with no definite home area.

The cheetahs were less favored by the continuing severe dry season. For them, hunting success depended on seeing prey and chasing it down. Herbivores hidden in riverine thickets were hard to see and impossible to chase. Duma did her best to provide food for herself and her three cubs, but it was a lean time. The mother cheetah spent most days resting and waiting—waiting for the rains to come, waiting for the herds to move back to the plains so she and her family could follow.

## Growing Up

The cheetah cubs seemed to enjoy life in spite of sometimes empty stomachs and the teething pains they suffered. The long-legged, slim cats did not look as if they were built for climbing trees, but that didn't stop the cubs from scrambling up any available tree trunk. Occasionally one of the cubs would climb into a tree only to find itself stuck, too frightened to get down. Then Duma would have to coax it with chirping noises until it was back on the ground like a sensible cheetah.

One day the three cheetah cubs found a snake curled up under a tree. Cautiously, they approached the strange creature. None of the cubs had ever seen a snake before, but they had learned something about the value of being wary. Unfortunately, they had not learned enough, because the snake was a spitting cobra. When the female cub reached out tentatively with one paw to investigate, the snake came alive. It reared up and spat. With a yelp of pain and surprise the cub jumped back. Her reactions were quick and most of the snake's venom had missed its target. But one drop had hit her eye.

Rubbing her eye with a paw didn't help. If anything, it made things worse. But of course the little cheetah didn't understand that. She could only feel

the terrible, burning sensation in her eye, a pain that nothing, not even her mother's gentle licking, could ease. Within an hour the eye was shut tight, the surrounding tissue discolored and swollen.

Such an injury is extremely dangerous. Not only is it possible for an animal to lose the sight of the affected eye, but it is also possible for the infection to spread to the other eye. A blind cheetah cub may survive for a time with a mother to provide for her, but she will never be able to hunt for herself. Duma's cub was lucky. Her body was strong enough to combat the effect of the venom. After two weeks the swelling lessened, and three weeks after the injury the eye was normal. The lesson had been frightening but effective. Neither the female cub nor her brothers would ever again bother a snake.

One animal living nearby was not afraid to bother snakes. This was a ratel, a tough little carnivore only two and a half feet long and eight inches tall. With thick fur that was black on its underparts and white on its back, the ratel looked something like a skunk-colored badger. Its habits were more like those of a mongoose, a small, fierce creature known for its snake-killing ability.

On the day after the cobra attacked the cheetah

cub, the ratel confronted the same snake. The ratel moved amazingly fast, jumping away just in time whenever the cobra struck. Finally, after many unsuccessful strikes, the snake began to tire and the ratel was able to catch it behind the head. The snake could not strike with its head immobilized and the ratel's powerful jaws quickly killed it.

In December, when the young Serengeti cats were nine months old, the rains began at last. As if to make up for the delay, the rain poured from the sky in unending torrents. There was far more water than even the parched land could absorb. Roads turned to muddy bogs. Within days, dry stream beds turned into swollen, raging rivers.

Animals who usually stuck close to home and out of sight were forced from flooded dens. Porcupines abandoned their burrows and huddled on rocky ledges. The unusually heavy rains provided a bonanza for a dozen different species of storks and other wading birds, who feasted on frogs from newly created marshes. Tiny round hedgehogs, their backs covered with short, sharp spines, appeared as if from nowhere to eat the abundant insects brought by the rains.

The rain was the signal the herds of wildebeests,

zebras and Thomson's gazelles had been waiting for. Their delayed migration to the eastern plains began. The animals moved along traditional routes that had been used for countless generations. This year, those routes took them through unusually full rivers with unusually strong current. Wildebeests are good swimmers, but many did not survive. The old, the sick, and several hundred calves who had been born early, while the herds remained in the woodlands, tired and drowned.

Duma the cheetah and her three cubs followed the herds. The cats' path was not dictated by some hereditary tradition, and the mother cheetah was free to select the driest route she could find. The cheetahs were often wet and uncomfortable, often in danger from roving lions, but never in serious danger of drowning.

The delayed, then intense short rains were not especially unusual for the Serengeti, a place that is characterized by unpredictable weather. Sometimes the rains come when they are expected. Just as often they are early or late. Sometimes they do not come at all. Every animal on the Serengeti is affected in some way by the rains. In some years, certain species benefit from the pattern of the seasons. In other years, those species suffer from another pattern, while dif-

ferent species benefit. If many wildebeests die one
year, perhaps few will die the next. Over the course
of centuries, everything tends to balance out. The
pattern of one year and the lives of individual animals
make very little difference.

Of course, the animals have no awareness of the
larger patterns. Each individual animal does its best
to survive under whatever conditions the Serengeti
offers.

Back on the plains, the cheetahs found conditions
more to their liking, especially after the steady rains
abated. By the end of January the rain came only in
the form of occasional showers. The ground dried out
sufficiently to provide firm footing for running cheetahs. There was plenty of prey too, not only the favorite Thomson's gazelles, but also ostriches.

No cheetah would think of attacking a full-grown
ostrich. Its huge size, powerful kick, and running
speed and endurance make it an unlikely target for almost any predator. But newly hatched ostriches are
something else. An ostrich nest may contain fifty or
more eggs (laid by several different female birds).
Some will not hatch—they may be stolen by baboons
and then abandoned, or by hyenas, predators with
jaws powerful enough to crush a thick eggshell. As

soon as the eggs hatch, the young may be taken by jackals, mongooses or hyenas. The surviving little ostriches, following their parents, are vulnerable to all kinds of predators if they become separated from the group. Fewer than half the ostriches which hatch survive long enough to grow to a safe size, but the many deaths mean survival for others, including cheetahs.

Duma was experienced at hunting ostrich chicks. She was seldom fooled by the mottled black and brown coloration that made them almost invisible when they crouched on the plain. The three cubs, however, often lost sight of a chick they were chasing if the little bird froze. At ten months of age, the young cheetahs still depended on their mother to feed them. They had not yet made kills of their own, and when they tried to assist Duma, more often than not they spoiled her hunting.

Nevertheless, the cubs displayed a more serious interest in hunting than they had ever shown before. They were almost full-grown now. The dark-colored male was larger than Duma, and the light-colored male about her size. The smaller male was less shy than before, and he now approached new situations fearlessly. The two male cubs remained inseparable. The female cub was considerably smaller than her brothers and was developing a respect for their size and strength, although she still dominated their games.

Like the young cheetahs, the leopard cubs were almost as big as adults. One day when the cubs were ten months old, the male lay on his back, stretched out along a branch of a sausage tree. Chui slept in the same tree. To any but the keenest eyes, it would have looked as if two adult leopards were peacefully sharing the same stretch of riverbank. Only very close observation would have revealed that the male was an adolescent who in a few months would be larger than his mother.

The female cub was nowhere in sight. But suddenly Chui looked up, listening intently. There was a rustling in the bushes nearby and then the cub ran up the tree trunk. Chui greeted her daughter affectionately, licking her all over. At first the cub seemed content to snuggle up next to her mother. But she did not remain there long. In a few minutes she ran down the tree again, headfirst, in the confident, graceful manner of an adult leopard. She leaped to the ground and looked up at her mother. When Chui did not respond, the cub grunted. Then the mother leopard stood up, stretched and followed the cub down the tree.

The cub led Chui through the dense underbrush to a tangled thicket about half a mile from the sausage tree. Plunging in, she emerged a few seconds later with a hare in her mouth. The cub had made her first kill, and it seemed as if she wanted to show it off to her mother. This mission accomplished, she quickly made her way back to the sausage tree carrying her prize.

The male cub was enormously interested in his sister's kill and he immediately tried to take it from her. Probably because Chui allowed him to take food from her, the cub seemed surprised and offended when his sister defended her kill by snarling. He whacked her in the head with his paw, but he kept his claws sheathed and made no further attempt to steal the food. Within a few days the male leopard had made a kill also. Still, both young leopards relied on Chui for most of their food. Only she was strong enough to handle large prey. Only she was skilled enough to be sure of hunting success even half the time. At the age of one year, the young leopards might have been able to survive on their own, but it would have been difficult. If they had lost their

mother at this point, their limited hunting skills
might have meant their starvation.

At the age of one year, the lion cubs would surely
have starved to death without their mother or the
other females of the pride. Lion cubs mature more
slowly than cheetahs or leopards. When they had
their first birthday, Simba's three surviving cubs
were just cutting their permanent teeth. All three
acted irritable. Their gums were sore and bleeding
and their noses were hot. In spite of their feverish
discomfort they were lucky to be alive at all. Two
other cubs near their age had died of starvation when
their mother proved less conscientious than Simba
about leading them to kill sites.

The male cub began to grow a mane. It didn't
look like much at first, but growth of hair proceeded
rapidly. In a few months he would have long
whiskers on the sides of his neck and a line of long,
bristly hairs from the top of his head all the way
down his neck. His adolescent looks were slightly
comical, giving little hint of the impressive creature
he would eventually become. His behavior didn't
help his image. He acted silly, chasing his own tail,
batting at grass, rubbing up against Simba, never able

to keep his attention on one thing for longer than a few minutes.

The females were different. Although in many ways they were still playful and kittenish, their span of attention was longer than their brother's. They seemed interested in hunting. They often watched their mother and the other lionesses as they stalked and ambushed prey. Their play seemed to be directed toward practicing what they saw.

Of course, male lions can and do hunt, and the young male would learn eventually. One day while he was walking alone through tall grass, he literally stumbled across the body of a giraffe. The animal had just died and the carcass was untouched, undiscovered by scavengers. The young lion had made a rare find indeed, and he seemed overjoyed. He rushed at the carcass and pounced, pawed it, pulled on the legs and ears and rolled around next to it, waving his legs and tail. From his behavior, an observer could not have told whether the cub recognized the giraffe as food, or whether he considered it merely an enormous toy.

But the cub was not to be left alone with his giraffe for long. Vultures circling overhead drew the attention of the other lions. Simba, three other adult

females, an adult male and four cubs arrived, and the giraffe was soon transformed from a toy to a meal. With such large prey, every cat had enough to eat and there was little of the squabbling that is usual among lions on a kill. After eating for ten minutes, Simba looked around, seemed to realize that her other two cubs were not there and trotted off to fetch them. Before the lions were finished with the giraffe, leaving the remains for the hyenas, jackals and vultures, every cat in the pride had a full meal.

On a rainy day in April, the thirteen-month-old cheetah cubs played near a narrow intermittent stream. One cub picked up a leaf in his mouth and paraded in front of his brother and sister. The other two watched him for a while, then, when they could resist the temptation no longer, began to chase him. Soon three young cheetahs rolled on the ground, tumbling over and over one another. In the growing excitement of the game the leaf was forgotten, and the cheetahs began to leap back and forth across the stream. This action startled dozens of frogs that had been resting on the muddy banks. The surprised frogs plopped into the water, one by one. And this was so interesting to the cheetahs that they stopped their leaping to sit at the stream's edge, staring in fascinated concentration at the frogs.

The cheetah cubs almost always played together, and their first serious attempts at hunting were made as a team also. The day after they watched the frogs their teamwork was rewarded. The three cats stalked a small herd of Thomson's gazelle females and fawns. Suddenly the two male cubs bounded at the herd, scattering the animals. While the attention of the mother gazelles was focused on this threat, the female cheetah cub quickly ran down a fleeing fawn.

She made the kill expertly, as if she had been hunting successfully for years. Her brothers immediately joined her, and the three cubs arranged themselves in a star formation around the carcass, allowing each cat elbowroom to feed. Amicably, the cubs ate their fill.

Cooperative hunting by the young cheetahs was an important step toward independence. None of the cubs was yet sufficiently skilled to hunt alone, but hunting together meant that they could survive without Duma. Throughout the spring rains, however, the whole family remained together, the mother and her young just as affectionate with one another as ever.

Duma seemed to know that her cubs were almost grown. She had given them a good start: They were healthy, they knew how to hunt, how to recognize danger and deal with it, how to behave with other cheetahs. In May the cubs' father, the large dark cheetah, appeared. He sat two hundred yards from the resting family, watching them, making no attempt to come closer. The next day, he approached. The cubs noticed, tensing visibly. The male slowed his approach, lowering the front part of his body on his elbows in a submissive gesture. In spite of this, the dark male cub lunged at him. He jumped away, slowly circled the group, then walked off.

Duma had not reacted to the presence of her mate, but she was totally aware of him. Several hours later, as the cubs played, she left them, following in the path of the male. She spent almost a week with the big cheetah, and when she returned to the cubs, she was pregnant again.

In her absence the cubs had killed three times. Clearly, they no longer needed her. In three months Duma would have a new litter to care for. It was time for mother and cubs to part for good. And so one day, as the Serengeti summer began, Duma set off in one direction and the three cubs set off in another. If they realized that they would not see each other again they did not seem unhappy. Their parting was natural and inevitable, like the seasons of the Serengeti.

It was time for the leopard cubs to leave their mother too, but the manner of their parting was quite different from the cheetahs'. One day all the cheetahs were together. The next, Duma and her cubs were permanently separated. With the leopards, the separation was more gradual, perhaps because each cub would live alone as soon as it left Chui.

The two leopard cubs began to spend more time by themselves. First the male went off for two nights. Then his sister left for a week. When she came back, she stayed with her mother for several days, then went off again. This pattern continued for three months, while each cub gained the confidence it would need to be a solitary adult leopard.

The female cub was the first to make a permanent separation from her mother. At the age of sixteen months, she was an adult, as large as Chui, as capable a hunter, and with the same need to live an independent life. Within a few months she would be ready to breed, to raise cubs of her own. Now the first stirrings of the need to find a mate arose in her and the urge to leave her mother's territory grew too strong to ignore.

For her part, Chui was ready to have her daughter leave. To the mother leopard the female cub was no longer a baby that needed protection but another adult female leopard, a rival within her territory. When the time for separation came, the break between mother and daughter occurred easily. The young female left to seek a life of her own.

Chui remained tolerant of the male cub for a longer time. Slower to mature than his sister, for a long while he seemed to lack the urge to be on his own. He enjoyed continued contact with his mother, snuggling up to her in the trees like an infant, although he was now much larger than she.

When the cub was eighteen months old, a break of sorts occurred. He stopped returning to his mother's favorite sleeping trees and no longer spent two or three days at a time in Chui's company. However, he did not seek his own territory. He continued to hunt in his mother's home area, apparently with Chui's approval. When he met his mother on a kill, Chui still allowed her son to take the meal away from her without so much as a growl.

A short while later the final break came. An older

male leopard began to visit Chui's river territory. In the evenings he called, making a strange harsh noise that sounded something like sawing wood. Chui answered his calls and, after a few evenings of "conversation," went to meet him. The courting couple would remain together for a time, sharing food and sleeping trees, playing like kittens. Now there was no room in the territory for Chui's full-grown cub. The cub seemed to realize this the first time he caught a glimpse of the male and so, finally, like his sister, he left his mother's home to find his own place on the Serengeti.

# Chapter Four

# Independence

Long after the young cheetahs and leopards were living on their own, the lion cubs remained dependent
members of the pride. The highly social life-style of
lions, unique among cats, allowed for a much longer
growing-up period for Simba's young. The burden of
caring for cubs did not rest on the mother alone, but
to some extent was shared by other adult females and
adult males as well. When cubs were small, they
were permitted to nurse from any lactating female in
the pride. When their mother went off by herself, the
cubs were protected by the presence of other adult

lions. When the cubs were older but still too small to fight successfully for a portion of a kill, the grown males in the pride often shared their meat with the youngsters. (Of course, as the cubs grew better equipped to fight for a piece of the kill, the grown males displayed a decreasing willingness to share with them.)

There was another important reason behind the lion cubs' long period of dependency—it took a long time to learn the complex social life-style of lions. Each cub had to learn how to behave with every other cat in the pride, how to react to strange lions, the limits of the pride's home area and, perhaps most important of all, how to hunt as part of a team.

When Simba's cubs were eighteen months old they were still very much youngsters in terms of their place in the pride. They were clearly smaller and less heavily muscled than the adults. The male cub had somewhat more mane than he had sported at the age of one year. Now it was apparent that within a year or so his mane would be a luxuriant, rich deep brown. He would be a large and forceful lion. Already, he dominated his sisters and the other cubs. But he was not yet mature enough to be a threat to the three adult males of the pride.

Shortly after sunset one evening, the three cubs accompanied Simba and another lioness on a hunt. The female cubs behaved as if they were out for a relaxing moonlight stroll. The male was more playful, bumping into his sisters, batting at his mother's flanks. After a while Simba turned and bared her teeth in a mild threat, seemingly warning the cub not to spoil the hunt.

The lions padded on, the male cub temporarily subdued. All the cats saw the prey at the same time—a lone zebra standing in the open. The moonlight was bright, there was little cover and the zebra was too far away to chase. The cats crouched, miraculously becoming nearly invisible in the short, dry grass. One of the female cubs began to move forward and to the right, stalking slowly, carefully. When the zebra turned its head in her direction, she froze, not moving a muscle until the animal turned away. She had watched the lionesses many times and now could imitate their patient stalking. Meanwhile, Simba approached to the left of the zebra. The other three cats moved straight forward, taking a few steps at a time, then flattening themselves against the ground.

The zebra noticed the three lions, possibly because the male cub was not sufficiently careful about hiding himself. The zebra watched the cats intently, not yet running, but prepared to do so if the predators came too close. It did not see the female cub approaching so stealthily from the right. When it finally fled, the zebra nearly ran into the young lioness, who rushed forward and grabbed it with one paw on the zebra's back, the other on its chest. Grasping the zebra's neck in her jaws, the cub tried to bring it down. She lacked both the strength and the experience. But the other cats rushed up and bowled the prey over. Simba quickly made the kill.

It would not be long before all three cubs, even the reluctant male, could kill their own prey. Even so, they still had much to learn before they were completely grown up. The three continued to play more than the adult lions, and play continued to serve important functions for them. Through play, the cubs practiced adult behavior, developed their muscles, learned about social relationships in the pride and explored the Serengeti around them.

Late one afternoon the three cubs played together on a kopje. Seemingly unaware of their large size, they chased each other madly over the rocks like tiny kittens first discovering their remarkable agility. A sudden noise in a thicket made the cubs freeze. The rustling came again. Without hesitation, the cats dived into the bushes. The next sound to come from the thicket was a clacking noise. The cubs had found a porcupine and the rodent was warning them to stay away by rattling its quills.

The warning went unheeded by the impetuous cubs. To the young male, the porcupine looked like perfectly good prey. In some parts of Africa where large prey is scarce, lions have made a specialty of hunting porcupines, learning to roll the rodents on their backs and avoid the quills. The Serengeti lions, however, have little need to bother with small animals and usually cannot deal with porcupines. The male cub reached out to subdue the rodent with a paw and his mouth at the same time. In an instant, a quill hung from his paw and three more protruded from his muzzle. With a cry of pain, he jumped back, bumping into one of his sisters. Then all three cubs turned tail and ran.

As he ran, the young lion dislodged the quill in his paw. Then he sat down and used his paws to remove the quills from his face. Although he tore his skin, he managed to take out all three quills. He was very lucky. A lion can easily be crippled by a porcupine quill in a foot, or prevented from opening its mouth by a quill in a jaw. Unremoved quills can cause infection, swelling and terrible pain. Lions injured by porcupines may die slowly and painfully by starvation. But now Simba's cubs would be safe from this danger. All had seen just what porcupines could do, and they would certainly show more respect for the rodents in the future.

As another summer dry season continued on the Serengeti, the ostriches began their courting. Just when most of the animals were at their most lethargic, their energy sapped by the heat and lack of water, the big birds were at their most active. In preparation for the breeding season, the male ostriches' featherless legs and necks had turned bright red and their black and white plumage had grown exceptionally glossy. Now they displayed to the hens by crouching low to the ground, with outstretched, trembling wings. They waved their necks from side to side. Sometimes they called, making a loud booming noise.

An accomplished ostrich dancer might attract several drab brown hens, who would whirl around him, fluttering their wings and lowering their heads. All the hens who mated with the same male would lay their eggs in the same nest, which was no more than a shallow hole scraped in the ground, sometimes right out in the open. Often, however, a careless hen would lay an egg wherever she happened to be at the time and then abandon it.

Finding such an abandoned ostrich egg one day, the male lion cub rolled it around for a while, playing with it like a ball. Then, almost experimentally, he bit it hard. To his surprise, it opened, and he hungrily lapped up the contents. From then on, Simba's son looked for ostrich eggs. He even grew brave enough to chase a brooding bird off a nest and steal an egg or two. Although an ostrich egg is as big as two dozen chicken eggs, it does not make much of a meal for a lion. Nevertheless, a lion with a special talent like opening thick-shelled eggs is less likely to starve than a lion with less creative ways of finding food.

As usual, the summer dry season brought twenty or more elephant bulls to the area around Seronera. Like so many other animals, they sought the water in the Seronera River when most of their usual water holes had dried up. Like the other animals too, the elephants needed the vegetation that survived near the permanent water source. Each elephant needed as much as five hundred pounds of food every day. To get it, many of them pushed over trees with their trunks and tusks.

As always, the devastation caused by the elephants was staggering. And as always, park officials argued over what to do about it. Some claimed that elephants killing trees was part of a natural cycle in which humans should not interfere. Besides, they argued, there was sufficient growth of new trees to replace those killed by elephants. Other people said that the elephants were destroying trees at a faster rate than new trees grew. In addition, they claimed, the elephants were spoiling the appearance of a beautiful area, one that was most accessible to tourists, and one that supported many animals that were rare in other parts of the park, including leopards.

Chui was one leopard who did not mind the elephants. She was used to them, knew enough to avoid them, and simply went about her usual way of life. Her two cubs had left, and she was temporarily sharing her territory with a male. In a few months she would have a new litter.

Chui's daughter had not gone far. A few miles up the river she had found an unoccupied area to her liking and established her territory there. She too was unconcerned about the elephants, having learned when she was small to give them a wide berth. And like her mother she had found a mate. By the time Chui's litter was born, her daughter would also have cubs.

The young male leopard did not remain so close to home. He had been unable to find an area nearby that both pleased him and did not already have a resident male leopard. He began to travel northward, moving slowly, advancing no more than two or three miles a night. He hunted small game, usually at dawn or dusk, and generally spent the hottest part of the day resting in any cover he could find.

After two weeks of wandering, the leopard arrived at Banagi on the bank of the south fork of the Grumeti River. Before the Serengeti National Park was established, a part of the area was a game reserve with headquarters at Banagi. The Banagi settlement is largely deserted, but when the leopard arrived, the small laboratory there was in use. A scientist studying the behavior of Thomson's gazelles in the northern part of the park had made Banagi his base of operations. The leopard did not mind the man's presence. He had seen humans before, tourists at Seronera. While he did not seek close contact with people, he did not fear them either. For his part, the zoologist welcomed the leopard. The beautiful cat was a pleasure to watch, even when it was doing nothing but reclining in a tree. The man hoped the cat would stay, but he suspected it would not.

At the end of the dry season not a drop of water remained in the Grumeti River. Most of the migratory animals had left and hunting was poor. Banagi was, for the moment, a rather uninviting place for a leopard. Perhaps if the leopard had arrived at some other time and established himself in the territory, he would have remained through the leanest part of the year. But for Chui's son at this time there was no reason to stay. He crossed the dry riverbed and moved on, this time traveling westward, following the river.

The leopard crossed the Musabi Plain. He was now in the western part of the park, the section known as the Corridor. The Corridor is a narrow extension of the Serengeti National Park into the surrounding area of heavy human settlement. All the animals of the Serengeti National Park are supposed to be safe from hunting, but in the Corridor poaching—illegal killing of animals—is a serious problem. Local people ignore the park boundaries and enter the Corridor to set traps or shoot animals. The people are poor and can earn much more money by selling meat and skins than they can by farming small plots. The Corridor is too large and too far from Seronera for the few park rangers to have much influence.

Naturally, the leopard did not know he had entered a dangerous place. Nor could he know that he was about to move into an even more dangerous area—outside the park. To local people used to living off the land, the artificial boundaries of a national park mean very little. To the animals, park boundaries mean nothing at all. The area that scientists call the Serengeti Ecological Unit—the region big enough to maintain the Serengeti's animals and plants in natural balance—contains about ten thousand square miles, or twice the area of the Serengeti National Park.

By the time the leopard reached the place where the north fork and the south fork of the Grumeti River join, the short rains had started and water rushed swiftly through the riverbed. Rather than cross the fast-flowing and suddenly deep water, the cat turned northeast, following the river's north fork. Within a few days the leopard had moved out of the park. If he had kept moving in the same direction, sticking close to the river, he would eventually have

reentered the park. But he liked the habitat he had found and there were no other leopards nearby. Unfortunately, there was very little wild prey either. In the heavily settled, unprotected area, most of the game animals had been killed or had moved away. And so, the cat with insufficient fear of man did not hesitate to visit human settlements in search of food. On his first foray he killed a goat.

Hunting domestic animals was ridiculously easy, so two days later the leopard returned to the same village for another meal. This time, however, the owner of the flock was waiting. The cat had no chance. As soon as the leopard appeared the man fired his rifle. With one shot the leopard's short life was ended.

The three cheetah cubs remained together for several months after leaving their mother. Through the long dry summer, hundreds of visitors on game-viewing drives through the Serengeti were treated to the sight of three cheetahs romping or resting together. Several dozen lucky tourists had the opportunity to watch the cats hunt. Everyone remarked on the cheetahs' marvelous cooperation and their incredible power and grace as they sped after their prey. All three cats were beautiful and healthy. Duma had successfully raised them to take their places on the wild Serengeti.

Duma was far less successful with her next litter. When her four cubs were six days old, she left them briefly to drink at the river. She didn't know that hyenas had discovered the den. As soon as she was gone a hyena went right to the thicket and killed and ate the cubs.

When she returned, Duma seemed to sense what had happened even before she checked the den. If she felt sadness at her loss, she was adapted for dealing with it. She was ready to mate again and within a month she was pregnant.

The loss of an entire litter is a common occurrence among predators. Thus cat populations do not grow too large for the environment. Cats compensate for the high death rate of cubs by having relatively large numbers of young at one time. Often, too, a cat will, like Duma, breed again almost immediately when a litter is lost. Since cubs do not require fresh vegetation and the protection of a large herd, they can safely be born at any time of year.

The populations of prey animals like wildebeests,

impalas and gazelles are kept in balance by a different mechanism. These herbivores are tied to specific breeding cycles. Most young are born at around the same time of year. Young are generally born singly, and if a mother loses her calf, she will not be ready to breed again until the next season. Because an enormous number of young prey animals fail to survive, the species depends for maintaining its numbers on most adult females in a large population breeding every single year.

The following January found Duma's twenty-two-month-old cubs still together. But that situation would soon be changed. The young female was restless. Often while her brothers napped she paced, calling constantly in a *chirring* voice. She was ready to breed. Still she seemed torn between conflicting desires—the wish to go off on her own to find a mate and the wish to remain in the comfortable, familiar companionship of her brothers.

In the end the problem was solved for her by the appearance of an adult male cheetah. Attracted by the female's calling and her scent, he approached, *chirping*, inviting her to follow him. After only a moment's hesitation she did so. For the next week the two cheetahs courted. They were together all the time, keeping up an almost constant stream of *chirrs* and *chirps*, sounding more like birds than cats. They chased each other, dashing madly across the plain, as the female had done with her brothers when they were kittens. When she padded about aimlessly, the male followed her. Sometimes she stopped and rolled over on her back, hitting her mate softly with her paws when he came to sniff or lick her.

The cats mated several times and the young female conceived her first litter. Then her attitude toward her mate changed. She was less inviting, less playful. Her slaps became more serious, and she often growled at him. He was less interested in her as well. After a while he drifted away.

Three months later, when the young female was just over two years old, her cubs were born in a thicket very like the one in which she herself had been born. Because she had remained in the territory she had shared with her brothers, it was inevitable that she should meet her littermates again. On an afternoon when her cubs were very small, the female rested outside the den, taking advantage of a brief

period of sunshine between rain showers. Her two brothers, out for a stroll, saw her. Recognizing their sister at once, they bounded over, clearly anticipating a joyous reunion.

But instead of a friendly greeting the males received a stern warning. The female charged at them, growling. The threat was unmistakable and the brothers did not persist, but turned and trotted away. The female cheetah behaved as she did not because she had forgotten her brothers, but because she had cubs to protect. She no longer had time for frivolous games. Her new responsibilities had made her, like her mother, a mature Serengeti cheetah.

The cheetah brothers would mature later, probably not mating for the first time until they were three or four years old. Even then, they might remain friendly with each other. One might go off with a female for several weeks at a time, but the bond between the brothers would probably remain strong. Very possibly, the two would always join up again, lifelong companions on the Serengeti.

Unlike ostriches, most of the Serengeti's birds breed during the rainy season, when insect food for protein-hungry young is most abundant. Generally the birds begin their courtship and nest-building activities in November or December at the start of the short rains. But in some years, when the rains are not especially intense or when they fail altogether, the birds delay their breeding until the start of the long rains in March. So it was this year, when the short rains began on schedule but petered out after only a couple of weeks. Birds who had begun courting stopped abruptly, to begin again in March.

The long rains were abundant. Ground-nesting birds like francolins and guinea fowl, who need the cover of tall grass, had an especially successful nesting season. Most birds managed to raise two broods, as if making up for their inability to nest a few months earlier. Weaver birds nested in great colonies, their intricately made nests covering their favorite trees. Kori bustards, large, heavy ground-dwellers, courted, the males making loud booming noises to announce territorial ownership and attract females. Sunbirds, starlings, swallows, flycatchers, hoopoes, rollers, bee eaters, kingfishers, barbets, larks—hundreds of species, millions of individual birds—nested on the Serengeti. Birds of prey—dozens of species of hawks and owls—raised young too, taking advantage of the breeding success of other birds, small mammals and reptiles to provide food for their own young. That March the Serengeti seemed bursting with birds.

That March also, the young Serengeti cats were two years old. For leopards and cheetahs, already started on independent lives, the beginning of their third year meant little. But for young lions it meant the transition from youngsters to subadult members of the pride. Their mother no longer led them to kills. In fact, Simba was beginning to sever her ties with her cubs. For the first time since the cubs were born, she came into heat and was ready to mate again. She would soon have another litter and the whole long process of raising young lions would start over.

Other adult lions in the pride were less tolerant of the two-year-olds than they had ever been before. The males treated them as adults at kills, no longer allowing them the eating privileges of young cubs. Simba's children had to compete like grown lions for their share. The adult females no longer permitted them to play with small cubs, and sometimes behaved with hostility toward them for no apparent reason.

This was an especially critical time in the lives of the young lionesses, for their behavior as subadults would very likely determine whether they would remain with the pride. If they acted nervous and unsure of themselves in the face of hostility, the adult lions would be encouraged to step up their attacks, treating Simba's daughters as if they were strangers and eventually driving them from the pride. But if they ignored the snarls and mock charges and unsheathed claws, the attacks would eventually diminish and they would be accepted by the other lions as full adult members of the pride.

For their brother, the outcome of the other lions' hostility would be the same no matter how he reacted. Like all male lions, he would begin to test his strength and daring against the pride's established males. And like all lions his age, he would be defeated by his own inexperience before he could mount a serious challenge. Forcible hints from the adult lions, combined with his own growing desire to explore the outside world, would drive him from the pride to lead a nomadic life. Only when age and experience and possibly the help of another lion in the same situation gave him the ability to wrest control from the leaders of another pride would he return to the social type of existence in which he grew up.

This system by which all young males and some

young females are forced to leave the pride has an important advantage for the species. It prevents closely related animals, for example a brother and sister, from mating, thereby reducing the numbers of weak, inbred young. Naturally, lions are not aware of the consequences of their social system. It evolved during the course of thousands of years because those lion prides that practiced it thrived while those that did not were weakened and eventually died out from inbreeding.

The three young lions still had a few things to learn. Life on the Serengeti held some surprises for the almost-grown cats. For example, they had seen rhinos many times and knew very well to keep away from them. A rhinoceros, with its vast bulk, thick skin, sharp horn and quick temper, is more than a match for a lion. But Simba's cubs had never seen a baby rhino until a rainy April morning when they went for a walk. The baby was quite small, with no hint of a horn, seemingly easy prey for three substantial young lions. One of the females began to stalk, when suddenly the mother rhinoceros appeared, galloping in the cubs' general direction with lowered head. The cats turned and scattered, running away as fast as they could. Adult lions would have known that a mother rhinoceros is very protective of her baby, never allowing it to stray very far. Certainly, adult lions would have investigated to make sure the mother was not around before deciding on a rhino calf as prey. Next time, Simba's cubs would be more careful.

For another six months following their second birthday the cubs continued to learn new lessons about their environment and to sharpen their hunting skills. At the age of two and a half they still had difficulty killing large prey by themselves, but all could hunt well enough to survive. The two females, calm and confident by nature, found that they were no longer targets of the other lions' hostility. They would remain with the pride, probably as close companions for their entire lives.

Just as the females' situation was resolved in one way, their brother's was inevitably resolved in the opposite way. At the age of two and a half, Simba's son left the pride forever. Not yet full-grown, he was already a large, handsome cat. His luxuriant mane would continue to grow and darken. But in spite of his impressive appearance, the first few weeks on his own were difficult for the young lion. He wandered

the Serengeti with no destination. Strange lions roared, warning him to keep out of their prides' territories. No other lions were available for companionship or for providing food. For the first time in his life, the lion was alone, dependent on himself only.

For eight days after leaving his pride Simba's son did not eat. He tried to hunt but was unable to catch anything. He rapidly lost his well-fed appearance. His skin hung loosely on his large frame and his ribs began to show.

On the ninth day he stalked two warthogs feeding in tall grass. Impatient to find a meal, the lion rushed at them too soon and the warthogs ran off in opposite directions. But the lion was too hungry to give up. He charged after one of the warthogs only to see the animal dive into its burrow. Still unwilling to quit, the lion clawed at the burrow entrance, furiously scattering dirt, enlarging the hole until he could enter. At last his hunting efforts were rewarded as his teeth fastened on the warthog's rump and he dragged the squealing, enraged animal out of the burrow. The warthog still had plenty of fight left in it but it was no match for the determined hungry lion. In a few minutes the warthog was dead and within two hours very little of it remained, even for the vultures.

## Serengeti Cats

Over the next few months the young lion became adept at digging warthogs out of their burrows. Of course, he sometimes managed to catch other prey, and he sometimes relied on his talent for opening ostrich eggs, but he was most successful at warthog hunting. Thus the lion would not only live, he would thrive until the next year, when he would be old enough and strong enough to take over a new pride of Serengeti lions.

*Chapter Five*

# The Future
# for Serengeti Cats

The Serengeti National Park is the home of approximately one thousand lions. This is the largest concentration of lions anywhere in the world. Simba and her cubs can expect to live for fifteen years or more in a protected environment with plenty of food and companionship.

For Chui and the Serengeti's 600 or so other leopards, and for Duma and the park's 250 other cheetahs, the immediate future is bright too. The Serengeti and other wildlife reserves are major tourist attractions. Tourism is an important source of income for many countries, and for poor nations like Tanzania it is vital. So there is an economic motive as well as a conservation motive involved in the creation and maintenance of national parks.

Unfortunately, the continued existence of the parks is not assured. The great majority of the poorest people in Tanzania and other East African countries earn no money from tourism. To them, wildlife is a source of income only if they can hunt the animals and sell the meat and skins. National parks take away land they could otherwise farm. And with human populations growing rapidly, there is constant pressure on governments to *decrease* the size of game parks, opening up more land to human settlement, instead of increasing park size to include entire ecological units and creating new parks as well.

There is also another problem for the wildlife reserves. More than twenty thousand people visit the Serengeti every year. These visitors bring in money, helping to pay for the park's operation. For most of them, seeing the Serengeti with its remarkable wildlife is a unique experience. It turns visitors into conservationists, determined to preserve wild Africa. And yet by their very numbers, the tourists can destroy it. The Serengeti is a fragile environment, easily damaged by automobile tracks and garbage dumps. With the stream of visitors increasing every year, the Serengeti has no time to recover from such damage.

In spite of the problems, the Serengeti cats' populations seem to be holding steady within the park. Outside the protected areas, the cats' prospects for survival are slim. Lions once ranged throughout Africa and through Asia as far east as India. As human settlement spread, large prey disappeared and so did lions. When lions tried to prey on domestic cattle they were killed. Three-hundred-pound predators living in groups simply cannot coexist peacefully with human settlers. Today, outside of Africa, the wild lion is virtually extinct. In Africa the lion's range has shrunk considerably and is still shrinking. Most wild lions live either in areas too remote and wild for human habitation or in wildlife reserves.

The cheetah's range was once similar to the lion's, although cheetahs were never very common. No doubt their specialized method of hunting made many places unsuitable homes for them. The sprinting cats quickly disappeared as people took over their territories. Except for small local populations, such as two hundred cats in a remote desert area of eastern Iran, most of the wild cheetahs in the world today are in Africa. With the total number of cheetahs in Africa estimated at five thousand, most experts consider the cheetah a seriously endangered species.

The leopard, most adaptable of the Serengeti cats, once had a range including all the areas occupied by the lion and cheetah and areas far beyond to the north and east. Like the other large cats, leopards are not tolerated by most human settlers and many leopard populations have been wiped out. Unlike other large cats, however, leopards have survived in some places in spite of efforts to eliminate them. A solitary life-style, willingness to prey on just about anything available, and silent strength and agility have enabled some few leopards to survive at the very edges of human settlements.

Outside protected reserves, the Serengeti cats' best chance for survival lies in zoos. Modern zoo people have recognized the need for zoos to be more than animal displays. They know that for many species, captive breeding is the only way to prevent extinction.

Breeding lions has never been a problem. As long ago as 850 B.C. Assyrian kings kept lions in captivity. With little knowledge of animal needs and behavior on the part of the ancient zookeepers, and undoubtedly under poor conditions, lions successfully bred and reared their young. Today, healthy, well-fed zoo lions breed almost too successfully. Many litters of four, five or six survive to adulthood. If there is any problem at all, it is finding enough zoo space to house all the lions.

Leopards breed reasonably well in captivity, although they are not nearly as prolific as lions. Cheetahs, however, present something of a challenge. They have long been kept in captivity. In some places, noblemen used to keep trained cheetahs to hunt antelope. But the cats were always wild-caught. Even an Indian prince who kept more than a thousand cheetahs was unable to induce them to breed.

Not until 1946 were cheetahs born in captivity, and even then the mother rejected the cubs. Twenty years more passed before captive-born cheetah cubs were reared by their own mother. Today, zoos try a number of different techniques, such as giving cheetahs enormous enclosures to allow room to run, and separating male and female cheetahs except when the cats are ready to mate. The birth of a litter of cheetahs is still a rare event in a zoo, but happily it is becoming more common. Within a few years there may be a healthy, growing population of zoo-born cheetahs.

Today, more and more people are beginning to

look at wild animals in a new way. They no longer consider wildlife important only for its economic value to humans. Instead, they accept the idea that animals are fellow creatures with a right to their own existence. This attitude helps to create new and bigger wildlife reserves, supports expensive field research and breeding programs for endangered species and may someday lead to restocking depleted wilderness areas with captive-bred animals. In the end, the fate of lions, leopards and cheetahs depends on people. Only humans can insure a permanent place in the world for Serengeti cats.

ALICE SCHICK, a graduate of Northwestern University, worked for a time as a textbook editor before turning to writing for children. Her deep interest in animal behavior is evidenced in her previous science books, *Kongo and Kumba: Two Gorillas*, *The Peregrine Falcons*, and *The Siamang Gibbons: An Ape Family*. She also collaborated with her husband, Joel Schick, on *Viola Hates Music*, *Santaberry and the Snard* and, with Marjorie N. Allen, on *The Remarkable Ride of Israel Bissell As Related by Molly the Crow*. While doing the research for *Serengeti Cats*, Ms. Schick visited the Serengeti.

JOEL SCHICK has illustrated several books for children, including *The Gobble-uns'll Git You Ef You Don't Watch Out!*, *Who in the Zoo?* and *Joel Schick's Christmas Present*.

The Schicks live in Monterey, Massachusetts, with a dog, six cats and two gerbils.